I0107552

Keys to the Kingdom Workbook

by
R. S. "Bud" Miller, D.D.
Publisher
Betty Miller, D.M.
Author

www.BibleResources.org

Overcoming Life Series

Christ Unlimited — P.O. Box 850 — Dewey, AZ 86327   USA

Unless otherwise indicated, all Scripture quotations are taken from the <u>King James Version of the Holy Bible</u> (KJV).

<u>Overcoming Life Series:</u>

<u>Keys to the Kingdom Workbook</u>

ISBN 1-57149-007-8

Copyright © 1995-2013

R. S. "Bud" and Betty Miller

P. O. Box 850

Dewey, Arizona 86327

Published by

Christ Unlimited Publishing

P. O. Box 850

Dewey, Arizona 86327

Publisher: Pastor R. S. "Bud" Miller

Printed in the United States of America.

Contents

Christ Unlimited — P.O. Box 850 — Dewey, AZ 86327   USA

Personal Introduction

A lack of education will not hinder anyone from taking this course, and a doctor's degree will not help. However, one requirement that is necessary for this course to benefit the student is a total <u>commitment</u> to God. The Holy Spirit is our teacher, and we can learn if we come to God as little children. Being hungry to know God is a necessary prerequisite in order for this course to be of help.

If any of us are to receive truth, we must seek God, who is truth, with our whole hearts. We must seek Jesus first, then the knowledge of His Word will be revealed to us. Therefore, I want to emphasize once again the need to become as "a little child" in our approach to learning God's Word (Matt. 18:1-4; Jer. 29:13).

We need to come humbly before God, asking Him to remove any "know-it-all" attitudes, in order to be teachable. By laying down everything we thought we knew, we give God a chance to correct things we have believed that were wrong. Then we can begin to live the overcoming lives that God intended for His children to experience.

This workbook is part of a course based on the <u>Overcoming Life Series</u>, nine books taken from our first published book, <u>How To Overcome Through the Christ Unlimited</u>. That book, given to us under the anointing of the Holy Spirit, covers most of the basic things a Christian needs to know to get started on a victorious, overcoming walk with the Lord.

Christ Unlimited — P.O. Box 850 — Dewey, AZ 86327   USA

We have purposely kept this course simple for the average Christian who needs help in understanding how to study the Word and how to sort out principles and concepts when he, or she, reads the Bible; however, it also is for the seminary student. In addition, it is designed for students who desire to use it as a correspondence course. They can learn from it, even if they are totally alone and without a human teacher. The Holy Spirit always is there to teach us as we study about His Word.

On the other hand, groups with a teacher, or moderator, also can use this course to advantage. Our prayer is that, however this course is taken, each student will complete it a different person and be conformed more into the image of Christ our Lord.

Bud and Betty Miller

Keys to the Kingdom Workbook

Section One

"How To Use the Keys"

Keys to the Kingdom Workbook
Section One: "How To Use the Keys"
Expository Introduction

[Author's Note: This workbook is the fourth in the Overcoming Life Series, which includes nine books and workbooks. Lessons also have supplementary material. Answers are provided at the end of the workbook and do not have to be the exact wording in many cases. The student simply needs to make sure that he, or she, has caught the concept or principle from the Word of God.]

In the Bible, keys always represent authority. The "keys to the Kingdom of Heaven," then, are simply principles of authority found in the Word of God. These keys will enable us to operate in the authority of the believer and enter into the overcoming life. One verse concerning these keys is Matthew 16:19:

And I will give unto thee the keys of the kingdom of heaven, and whatsoever thou shalt bind on earth shall be bound in heaven, and whatsoever thou shalt loose on earth, shall be loosed in heaven.

What that verse means is that we can loose only what has already been loosed or bound in Heaven. This is contrary to doctrinal teaching prevalent in the Church today which says that believers have the sovereignty to arbitrarily bind or loose things according to our wills and God will enforce it. That teaching actually is opposite to the meaning of the verse above.

Christ Unlimited — P.O. Box 850 — Dewey, AZ 86327   USA

What God has forbidden or bound, we cannot use.

We cannot go against the principles or laws of God. However, there are <u>keys</u> we can use that give us authority as believers. What God has given in His Word has been loosed in the earth and can be used. Christians need to search God's Word to see what needs to be loosed in their lives and what needs to be bound. In other words, what do we need to <u>enforce</u> or <u>receive</u> in our lives that God has already provided for us.

Some of the things we can see immediately that have been "loosed" in the earth are: salvation (total redemption for the sin nature and for our sins), healing of the body, the fruit of the Spirit, the Kingdom of God.

Some of the things bound in Heaven (by Jesus' work on the cross) that now can be bound on earth are: the work of the devil in our lives, poverty, sickness and disease, and spiritual death. However, any of these, or other things accomplished by Jesus are only effective in our lives if we <u>receive</u> or <u>enforce</u> them. For example:

*The devil will not stay bound in anyone's life who is not totally committed to God.

*Salvation and release from spiritual death (eternal separation from God) is only operating in the life of someone who has received Jesus. That person has "loosed" salvation on earth for himself by his acceptance of the Lord as Savior.

*Healing is the right of all Christians; however, many do not "loose" it in their lives by receiving it from the Lord.

Luke 12:32 says it is God's good pleasure to give us the Kingdom, but He cannot give us something we will not receive.

When we become born again, we are translated into His Kingdom (Col. 1:12,13). Christians should understand that being born again means not only being adopted into the family of God, but enlisting in the army of God and becoming a citizen of the Kingdom of God. We should not be living like spoiled brats crying because we cannot have everything we want, nor should we be living in poverty as if we had no kind, loving Father.

We should be:

*Living like "King's kids" in all of the rights and privileges of our family rank

*Undergoing training and discipline necessary to be good soldiers

*Learning all of the principles that will enable us to become good citizens and obedient children.

The six keys we will be studying in this workbook are:

1. Praying in tongues (Section One)

2. Praise and worship (2-5 will be covered in Section Two)

3. Prayer

4. Intercession

5. Travail

6. Fasting

Each of these keys, or tools of the Christian, has a specific purpose, but none of them will work if they are not used. These principles only work for born again believers who operate within the framework, or guidelines, shown us in the Word for using these keys.

The guidelines are very important. They are the <u>ground rules</u> or conditions on which the keys are designed to operate.

*First, we must bind or loose according to God's will. (1 John 5:14,15) To know His will, we must find one or more scriptures that state what His will is for a particular situation.

*Secondly, we can use these keys effectively only if our own wills have been submitted and committed to God. When we are willing to do whatever God wants, then He will reveal His will to us. Jesus Himself did not do anything, say anything, or make any decisions apart from the Father's will when He was on earth (John 5:30).

The daily prayer of every Christian should be, "Father, what do you want me to do today?"

This is not a mystical or unreasonable thing to do, nor is it just for those people in ministries. A layperson who has a secular job can pray this and then deal with daily matters according to the will of God. John 15:7 says that if we abide in Him and His words abide in us, we shall receive anything we ask for. But notice the two <u>ifs</u> in that statement: <u>If</u> we abide in Him, and <u>if</u> His words (His will) abide in us.

*Thirdly, we must ask things of God with the right motives. James 4:3 tells us that we do not receive when our motives and desires are wrong.

For example, even a wife asking God for her husband's salvation can ask with the wrong motives: "Oh, God! I can't stand him any longer. Save him, and ease my misery and hardship." In this case, she is only asking for her own benefit, not the husband's and not for God to save another soul.

When Jesus said to pray for those who despitefully use us (**Matt. 5:44**), He meant to pray for them out of a genuine compassion and concern, rather than praying to be rid of them or free of their disturbances. We will study more about prayer in the second section.

Key One: Praying in Tongues

The first lesson in this workbook will focus on a key that has been quite controversial in the last decades: speaking or praying in tongues. However, this is one of the Christian's most valuable tools.

Praying in tongues also is spoken of in the Bible by two other terms: "praying in an unknown tongue" and "praying in the Spirit" (1Cor. 14:14,15) This is the key that can make a real difference in whether or not a Christian will live the overcoming life.

When we pray in the Spirit, that means the spirit man is doing the praying. As created by God, man is tripartite: spirit (the real person who will step out of the body at physical death), the soul (mind, will, and emotions), and the body (the "earth suit" in which man is able to live and communicate in the material universe). The spirit being is praying in accord with and under the authority of the Holy Spirit. Also, praying in tongues is known as a Christian's "private prayer language."

Christ Unlimited — P.O. Box 850 — Dewey, AZ 86327   USA

When we pray in the Spirit, our minds cannot comprehend what our voices are saying; however, God understands because the Holy Spirit is initiating the prayers within us (1 Cor. 14:2). He knows exactly how and for what we should be beseeching the Father. Occasionally, the Holy Spirit may give us the interpretation of what we are praying, but this does not happen every time.

Some denominations and independent Christians do not believe speaking in tongues is for today because of a doctrine known as Dispensationalism that divides the ages of mankind into certain periods of time. This doctrine says that in each period, God deals differently with mankind, so that certain things are valid in one period but not in another. The people who do not believe in the gifts of the Spirit for today say those were released only for the beginning of our present "dispensation," which they call the age of grace.

However, the Bible says that Jesus never changes (Heb. 13:8). **Jesus Christ the same yesterday, and today, and forever.** What He did in the first century, He is still doing today — if we receive Him and allow Him to do these things in our lives. Miracles and healing are still available for the Church today if we will only believe.

The Word of God shows us that, even more than knowing the gifts of the Spirit are for today, Christians actually were <u>commanded</u> by Jesus to allow the Holy Spirit to operate His gifts through them. These things, such as praying in tongues, were supposed to be part of the normal Christian life. This command or directive is condensed, or capsulized, in what is known as "the Great Commission."

Christ Unlimited — P.O. Box 850 — Dewey, AZ 86327   USA

And he said unto them, Go ye into all the world, and preach the gospel to every creature. He that believeth and is baptized shall be saved; but he that believeth not shall be damned. And these signs shall follow them that believe: In my name shall they cast out devils; they shall speak with new tongues; They shall take up serpents; and if they drink any deadly thing, it shall not hurt them; they shall lay hands on the sick, and they shall recover.

So then after the Lord had spoken unto them, he was received up into heaven, and sat on the right hand of God. And they went forth, and preached every where, the Lord working with them, and confirming the word with signs following. Amen.

Mark 16:15-20

The main directive, or commandment, that Jesus gave His disciples (which extends to all believers since) was to take the Gospel to the ends of the earth (evangelism). He promised that supernatural signs would follow those who did this — which specifically included them that believe (all Christians who will follow this instruction).

The signs mentioned in those verses include casting out demons, speaking with new tongues, protection from deadly dangers, and laying hands on the sick to recover. The gifts of the Spirit which the Apostle Paul wrote about in 1 Corinthians 12 include even more signs available to the believer.

Acts 2:38,39 shows us that the Holy Spirit's gift of speaking in tongues is for all. In other words, it is a gift to the Body of Christ, manifested through any believer who will allow it. The Great Commission makes it very plain that the Lord does not send His followers out to minister without empowering them to meet any hindrance or attack of the enemy.

The phrase **take up serpents** is referring to dealing with demons. A few cultic churches have taken this verse literally and have ended up in presumption, tempting God by actually basing their salvation on whether they have faith enough to handle poisonous snakes and not be killed, rather than on the blood of Jesus.

Many missionaries in the last 150 years have been defeated or even died on foreign soil because they tried to take the Gospel into enemy territory without using the tools provided and without being empowered by the Holy Spirit. Even more Christians are defeated in their everyday lives for the same reason. Without the empowerment of the Holy Spirit, Christians cannot be overcomers.

Speaking with other tongues begins when one is baptized in the Holy Spirit, a separate event from conversion. Becoming born again is when the Holy Spirit enters a person upon invitation and, through imparting the life of God, He makes that person a "new creature" (2 Cor. 5:17). From then on, the Spirit indwells such a person (Rom. 8:9-11; 1 Cor. 6:19).

The disciples of Jesus received the Holy Spirit in the new birth while Jesus was still on earth following the crucifixion (John 20:22). But they were baptized (received empowerment) on the Day of Pentecost, after Jesus had ascended to Heaven (Acts 2:2-4).

Other Facts About Praying In Tongues

Being "baptized" in the Spirit is sometimes referred to as being filled with the Spirit, or as the <u>infilling</u> of the Spirit to distinguish this event from the <u>indwelling</u> of the Holy Spirit. <u>To be baptized</u> means to be totally immersed in water, or in this case, to be totally immersed in the Holy Spirit. <u>To be filled</u> means the full penetration of the Holy Spirit into a Christian's life.

The Apostle Peter said the Day of Pentecost experience fulfilled the prophecy through the prophet Joel that God would one day pour out His Spirit "on all flesh" (Acts 2:17,18; Joel 2:28,29).

To receive this baptism or infilling with the evidence of speaking in tongues, one must first be born again. Then one must <u>receive</u> the Holy Spirit by faith. God will not force a person to speak in tongues any more than He will force someone to get saved. Also, the Holy Spirit does not "take over" a person's voice and speak through them. The individual speaks forth words <u>as the Holy Spirit gives them utterance</u>, meaning that He gives the words to the spirits of men and women. Then they speak forth the words (Acts 2:4). Even those who believe this empowerment is for today sometimes fear that opening oneself up to this supernatural experience means losing control of oneself.

The way to get around this is to accept the fact that the Father in Heaven will not give us anything bad or false if we ask for His good and perfect gift (Luke 11:11-13). Once a person is born again, he can pray for the baptism and <u>allow</u> the Holy Spirit to fill him.

Christ Unlimited — P.O. Box 850 — Dewey, AZ 86327   USA

The only caution is for someone who has been involved in the occult, spiritism, or satanic operations (astrology, psychic readings, seances — even many movies, books, and video games). That person needs to repent of such things, renounce them in the name of Jesus, and sometimes, it is necessary to go to a minister for actual deliverance. Satan and fallen angels also have languages (false tongues), and history tells us of satanic oracles being spoken in non-earthly tongues. In seances, evil spirits use the voices of "channelers" or persons who give themselves over to demonic use.

However, a person in whom the devil has no foothold and who is truly saved and committed to the Lord will have no problems, and the Holy Spirit will be able to truly infill that person with the evidence of speaking in tongues (Acts 2:4, 19:6; John 1:33, 7:38,39).

Speaking or praying in tongues can sound like anything from a few stammering words or syllables to a full language. Sometimes the "tongue" is a foreign earthly language which the person did not know mentally but which the Holy Spirit manifests at a particular time for His particular purpose (Isa. 28:11; Acts 2:4,6).

Some people start out just praying or praising with a few sounds before their prayer languages fully manifest. If they get in prayer before the Lord and begin to pray in whatever syllables come forth, soon a full flow of words will be released from the spirit. Speaking in tongues is not understood by man, but by God.

Jesus intended for all of His followers to receive the Holy Spirit in His fullness (Acts 2:38,39), according to the Apostle Paul.

Christ Unlimited — P.O. Box 850 — Dewey, AZ 86327   USA

I would that ye all spake with tongues, but rather that ye prophesied: for greater is he that prophesieth than he that speaketh with tongues, except he interpret, that the church may receive edifying.

1 Corinthians 14:5

There are two kinds of "gifts of tongues:" (1) prayer languages given to every believer who is filled with the Holy Spirit, and (2) an unknown tongue through which a message is given by interpretation to the Church (1 Cor. 12:30). The second type often is linked with the gift of prophecy (Acts 19:6) or the gift of the word of knowledge, as we can see from New Testament accounts.

The prayer language gift of tongues is: an important part of a believer's prayer life and a great weapon against the devil. It is also a way in which to "edify" (or build up) a believer's inner man (1 Cor. 14:3,4) like a battery being recharged. Praying in the Spirit puts the devil and his demons at a great disadvantage, because they cannot understand what is being prayed and therefore are unable to prepare counterattacks.

For he that speaketh in an unknown tongue speaketh not unto men but unto God: for no man understandeth him; howbeit in the spirit he speaketh mysteries.

1 Corinthians 14:2

Christ Unlimited — P.O. Box 850 — Dewey, AZ 86327   USA

Praying (or especially, singing) in tongues can be used to overcome depression. The time we most need to pray in tongues is when we do not feel like it! Singing or praying in tongues can produce blessings. First Corinthians 14:15,16 show that praying or singing in tongues also can be giving thanksgiving or praise to God.

What is it then? I will pray with the spirit, and I will pray with the understanding also: I will sing with the spirit, and I will sing with the understanding also. Else when thou shalt bless with the spirit, how shall he that occupieth the room of the unlearned say A-men at thy giving of thanks, seeing he understandeth not what thou sayest?

Speaking in tongues brings revelation. Using our prayer languages can bring us into communion with the Holy Spirit in order to receive wisdom and knowledge concerning certain situations or people. Praying in the Spirit causes us to be able to pray about these situations in a way that is according to God's will as the Holy Spirit is prompting our prayers. Because we are not able in the natural to know all of the truth or all of the facts concerning situations, we could very easily pray something in English that would not be in God's will for that person or that situation. The "interpretation" of our prayers might be given to us as revelation, or spiritual knowledge, or prophecy, or understanding of doctrines.

Now, brethren, if I come unto you speaking with tongues, what shall I profit you, except I shall speak to you either by revelation, or by knowledge, or by prophesying, or by doctrine? ...If any thing be revealed to another that sitteth by, let the first hold his peace.

1 Corinthians 14:6,30

Praying in tongues is also very effective in intercessory prayer (prayer for others), as at times we do not know how to pray for them. This makes praying in the spirit a valuable tool not only in our behalf but for others as well.

Likewise the Spirit also helpeth our infirmities: for we know not what we should pray for as we ought: but the Spirit itself maketh intercession for us with groanings which cannot be uttered. And he that searcheth the hearts knoweth what is the mind of the Spirit, because he maketh intercession for the saints according to the will of God.

Romans 8:26-27

Speaking in tongues is linked with the ability to witness about Jesus properly and effectively (Acts 1:8, 2:4). Because such praying edifies the spirit, we can become bolder and more confident in the Lord after spending much time in this kind of prayer.

Lesson for Section One

[Author's Note: All Scripture references that answer these questions have been given. Please do not look at the answer page until you have answered the questions in your own words. This is an expository lesson to help you learn.]

I. Introduction to Keys to the Kingdom

A. What do keys in this verse in Matthew represent?

_____

And I will give unto thee the keys of the kingdom of heaven...

Matthew 16:19

1. Who gave believers these keys?

_____

Reference: Matthew 16:19

2. Then, in whose authority do we operate them?

_____

B. List the scripture reference for "binding and loosing."
(See expository introduction.)

_____

1. Where must things first be bound and loosed, according to the expository lesson?

_____

2. Who can do this?

_____

3. Name one thing that has been bound in Heaven.

_____

C. Why should Christians want to find and use Kingdom keys?

_____

_____

1. Can any human being use these keys? _____

2. What is the first prerequisite for using these keys?

_____

Reference: John 3:16

3. The expository introduction lists three conditions, in

Christ Unlimited — P.O. Box 850 — Dewey, AZ 86327   USA

addition to being born again, for the keys to the Kingdom to operate. Name these conditions.

a. _____

Reference: 1 John 5:14,15

b. _____

Reference: John 5:30

c. _____

Reference: James 4:3

4. Are all believers told to operate in the keys? _____

   a. How do we know this?

   _____

   b. What is Jesus' last directive to His disciples called?

   _____

   Reference: Mark 16:15-18

D. Name six keys to the Kingdom discussed in this workbook:

   1. _____

   2. _____

3. _____

4. _____

5. _____

6. _____

II. The First Key

A. An important key, a form of prayer that is a tremendous weapon available to all Christians, is: _____.

1. When we pray in tongues do we understand in our minds what we are praying?_____

a. What does speaking in tongues sound like?

_____

For with stammering lips and with another tongue will he speak to this people.

Isaiah 28:11

Now when this was noised abroad, the multitude came together, and were confounded, because that every man heard them speak in his own language.

Acts 2:6

b. Are the "other" tongues always earth languages? _____

2. Who does understand our prayers in unknown tongues?

_____

For he that speaketh in an unknown tongue speaketh not unto men, but unto God: for no man understandeth him; howbeit in the spirit he speaketh mysteries.

                              1 Corinthians 14:2

a. In addition to ourselves and other men, who does not understand our prayers? _____

b. How does this hinder the devil?

_____

3. What part of the believer really is praying?

_____

Reference: 1 Cor. 14:15

4. Does the Holy Spirit force the believer to speak? _____

5. What part does He play in speaking with other tongues?

_____

Reference: Acts 2:4

Christ Unlimited — P.O. Box 850 — Dewey, AZ 86327   USA

B. Is speaking in tongues by the Holy Ghost for today?

_____

Then Peter said unto them, Repent, and be baptized every one of you in the name of Jesus Christ for the remission of sins, and ye shall receive the gift of the Holy Ghost. For the promise is unto you, and to your children and to all afar off, <u>even as many as the Lord our God shall call</u>.

Acts 2:38,39

1. What directive did Jesus give that tells us we are to speak in tongues?

_____

Reference: Mark 16:15-18

a. According to Mark 16:17, signs shall follow the

_____.

b. Was "the Great Commission" given to us as well as to believers of the apostles' day? _____

2. Is Jesus the same today, and is God the same in every generation? _____
Reference: Hebrews 13:8

C. Looking at "the Great Commission" (Mark 16:15-18), we find that the Lord does not send us out to minister without His gifts and power. Some of the things His power was given to us for, as mentioned in those verses, are:

1. _____

2. _____

3. _____

4. _____

5. _____

D. The gift of tongues should be an important part of every Christian's prayer life as it gives us not only the power to become overcomers, but also is a great weapon against the _____. Some other benefits of praying in tongues are:

1. We can pray _____ as we are not solely dependent on our natural minds and understanding.

And he that searcheth the hearts knoweth what is the mind of the Spirit, because he maketh intercession for the saints according to the will of God.

Romans 8:27

2. The gift of tongues is given us to _____ or to build up our spirits.

But he that prophesieth speaketh unto men to edification, and exhortation, and comfort. He that speaketh in an unknown tongue <u>edifieth himself</u>; but he that prophesieth edifieth the church.

1 Corinthians 14:3,4

3. Praying in tongues is effective in _____
   prayer, as at times, we do not know how to pray.
   Reference: Romans 8:26-27

4. We glorify and _____ God by praying in the Spirit.

And they were all amazed and marvelled saying one to another, Behold, are not all these which speak Galileans? Cretes and Arabians, we do hear them speak in our tongues the wonderful works of God. ...For they heard them speak with tongues, and magnify God ....

Acts 2:7,11, 10:46

5. We receive _____ and _____
   when we speak in tongues.

Whom shall he teach <u>knowledge</u>? and whom shall he make to understand <u>doctrine</u>? them that are weaned from the milk, and drawn from the breasts. For precept must be upon precept, precept upon precept; line upon line, line upon line; here a little

Christ Unlimited — P.O. Box 850 — Dewey, AZ 86327   USA

and there a little: For with stammering lips and another tongue will he speak to this people.

Isaiah 28:9-11

6. Speaking in tongues is linked with boldness to _____.

But ye shall <u>receive power</u> after that the Holy Ghost is come upon you; and ye shall be <u>witnesses</u> unto me both in Jerusalem, and in all Judea, and in Samaria, and unto the uttermost part of the earth. . . . And they were all filled with the Holy Ghost, and began to speak with other tongues, as the Spirit gave them utterance .

Acts 1:8, 2:4

And when they had prayed, the place was shaken where they were assembled together; and they were all filled with the Holy Ghost, and they spake the word of God <u>with boldness</u>.

Acts 4:31

7. Speaking in tongues also is linked with _____.

And when Paul had laid his hands upon them, the Holy Ghost came on them; and they spake with tongues, <u>and prophesied</u>.

Acts 19:6

8. Singing and praying in tongues produces _____.
Reference: 1 Corinthians 14:14-16

Christ Unlimited — P.O. Box 850 — Dewey, AZ 86327   USA

9. Speaking in tongues is a _____ for unbelievers
and brings revelation to believers.
Reference: 1 Corinthians 14:6,30

Wherefore tongues are for a sign, not to them that believe, but
to them that believe not: but prophesying serveth not for them
that believe not, but for them which believe.

1 Corinthians 14:22

E. However, we are not to confine our praying to tongues only,
but to continue to pray in our _____.

For if I pray in an unknown tongue, my spirit prayeth, but my
understanding is unfruitful. What is it then? I will pray with the
spirit, and I will pray with the understanding also: I will sing
with the spirit, and I will sing with the understanding also.

1 Corinthians 14:14,15

F. Praying in tongues also is called by two other terms in the
Bible. What are these terms?
Reference: 1 Cor. 14:2,14,15

1. _____

2. _____

3. The term "the baptism in the Spirit" can also be expressed in what words?

_____

Reference: Acts 2:4, 4:31

    a. Who were the first people under the New Covenant to be filled or baptized, in the Spirit? _____
       Reference: Acts 2

    b. Name some of the languages in which people heard the apostles speak on the Day of Pentecost, as found in Acts 2:9-11.

_____

_____

G. There are two kinds or types of gifts of tongues. Name them.

   1. _____

   2. _____

_____

Reference: 1 Cor. 14:5; 1 Cor. 12:30

H. How can a person be sure he will not get something false when he speaks in tongues?

_____

If ye then, being evil, know how to give good gifts unto your children; how much more shall your heavenly Father give the Holy Spirit to them that ask him?

Luke 11:13

1. Can someone receive a false gift of tongues?

_____

2. If a person has been involved in the occult (New Age or satanism, psychic, and so forth), what should he do before asking for the baptism of the Holy Spirit?

_____

III. A Final Assignment for This Section:

A. Study 1 Corinthians 12-14 to Biblically understand the two gifts of tongues. The three chapters cover these aspects:

1. Chapter 12 discusses the ministry gifts and their relationship to the entire Body of Christ.

2. Chapter 13 discusses the means by which these gifts are to operate: His love.

3. Chapter 14 gives the Church the proper order in which the gifts are to be administered.

Christ Unlimited — P.O. Box 850 — Dewey, AZ 86327   USA

Wherefore, brethren, covet to prophesy, and forbid not to speak with tongues. Let all things be done decently and in order.

1 Corinthians 14:39,40

B. Personal experience

1. If a student has not been filled with the Spirit, he might want to seek this, either in prayer by himself or asking the study group leader or a pastor to pray with him.

2. The student then should practice praying in his prayer language until he understands the experience for himself.

Christ Unlimited — P.O. Box 850 — Dewey, AZ 86327   USA

Overcoming Life Memory Verse

The suggested memory verse for this section is:

But seek ye first the kingdom of God, and his righteousness, and all these things shall be added unto you.

Matthew 6:33

Christ Unlimited — P.O. Box 850 — Dewey, AZ 86327   USA

Review Outline, Section One

I. Transferred to a New Kingdom (Col. 1:12,13)

    A. The Keys to the Kingdom help us overcome

    B. Our Father wants to give us the Kingdom (Luke 12:32), which is:

        a. Healing, provisions, other blessings

        b. To experience Heaven now through the Holy Spirit

    C. Keys are necessary to "unlock" the Kingdom

        a. Must have a proper understanding of Kingdom principles

        b. Must know that the <u>keys</u> represent authority

    D. Foundation for use of keys: Revelation of who Jesus is (Matt. 16:16-19)

II. The Kingdom is made up of saints of all ages: Israel of the Old Covenant and the Israel of God (born-again believers) of the New Covenant (Gal. 6:16).

    A. The Church, or the Body of Christ is:

        1. Made up of all born-again believers

        2. A spiritual temple, not a physical one

        3. Held together by love

        4. Characterized by allegiance to Christ's Lordship

    B. The Church was given authority to rescue the captives (Luke 10:17-19)

III. Six Keys to the Kingdom of God

   A. Speaking in tongues

   B. Prayer

   C. Praise

   D. Intercession

   E. Travail

   F. Fasting

IV. The First Key: Prayer in Tongues

   A. The Great Commission tells us Christians are to speak in tongues (Mark 16:15-18).

      1. The baptism of the Holy Spirit is to enable us to minister in the power of the Spirit.

      2. Speaking in tongues is the evidence of the baptism (Acts 2:4).

   B. Praying in tongues also edifies our spirits (1 Cor. 14:3,4).

Christ Unlimited — P.O. Box 850 — Dewey, AZ 86327   USA

Review Outline Quiz, Section One

1. When we become born again, we are transferred from the kingdom of _____ to the Kingdom of_____.

2. Is the Kingdom of God a physical or a spiritual Kingdom?

   _____

3. Who are the citizens of the Kingdom of God?

   _____

4. Why do we need keys to the Kingdom? _____

5. What do the keys to the Kingdom represent?

   _____

6. What is the only basis for the use of keys to the Kingdom?

   _____

7. In what verses did Jesus tell His followers to speak in tongues?

   _____

Christ Unlimited — P.O. Box 850 — Dewey, AZ 86327   USA

8. Name the six keys listed in the review outline:

    a. _____

    b. _____

    c. _____

    d. _____

    e. _____

    f. _____

9. What is the evidence of the baptism of the Holy Spirit?

_____

10. How can we edify our spirits? _____

Keys to the Kingdom Workbook

Section Two

"Becoming an Overcomer"

The Keys to the Kingdom Workbook
Section Two: "Becoming an Overcomer"
Expository Introduction

[Author's Note: This workbook is the fourth in the Overcoming Life Series, which includes nine books and workbooks. Lessons also have supplementary material. Answers are provided at the end of the workbook and do not have to be the exact wording in many cases.]

In this section, we will discuss the remaining five keys to the Kingdom that were mentioned in Section One.

An important part of being a citizen of the Kingdom of God is learning how to rule and reign in this life with Jesus Christ. Understanding these six keys to the Kingdom and how to use them is essential to an overcoming life in Him.

The first key we discussed was prayer in tongues. The other five keys are:

*Praise and worship

*Prayer

*Intercession

*Travail

*Fasting

The Second Key: Praise and Worship

Usually, when people think of praise and worship, they link it to singing and playing praise music unto God. However, that is only one form of praise and worship. Having a grateful and thankful heart is definitely another way in which we can worship God, but the highest form of worship is our obedience to God. This type of worship is what brings about our victories.

Praise and worship will unlock the Kingdom of God to us. In looking at the praise of God in the Bible, we can see that Jesus praised the Father (Luke 11:2), the Old Testament saints praised Him (2 Chron. 20:22, among many other verses), and New Testament believers are admonished throughout the Gospels and epistles to praise the Lord. In the book of the Revelation of Jesus Christ, we are shown the prayers, praise, and worship that occurs in Heaven. We need to get used to praising Him down here, because all Heaven resounds constantly with His praises.

And a voice came out of the throne, saying, Praise our God, all ye his servants, and ye that fear him, both small and great. And I heard as it were the voice of a great multitude, and as the voice of many waters, and as the voice of mighty thunderings, saying, Alleluia: for the Lord God omnipotent reigneth. Let us be glad and rejoice, and give honour to him: for the marriage of the Lamb is come, and his wife hath made herself ready.

Revelation 19:5-7

In addition, the Bible says that even the stones would be raised up to praise God, if people stopped praising Him.

Christ Unlimited — P.O. Box 850 — Dewey, AZ 86327   USA

And he answered and said unto them, I tell you that, if these should hold their peace, the stones would immediately cry out.

Luke 19:40

Every creature will eventually "bow the knee" in worship (Phil. 2:10) to Jesus, the Son of God or God incarnate, who has been given authority over all things (Matt. 11:27, 28:18).

The opening line of The Lord's Prayer (Matt. 6:9; Luke 11:2), which Jesus gave us as an example of how to pray to the Father, involves praise and worship:

Our Father which art in heaven, Hallowed be thy name.

Every time we pray, we should begin by praising and worshipping our Father in Heaven.

Praise and worship goes along with thankfulness, or expresses our thankfulness to God for all He is and for all He does and has done for us. In fact, the Apostle Paul wrote for believers to praise God in all things (1 Thess. 5:18; Eph. 5:20). The emphasis in these verses, and the context of the verses, is on praise. The apostle did not mean to imply that attacks of the enemy or sickness and disease are the will of God for us! We are to discern what is from the devil and what is of God. However, in the midst of temptation and tribulation, we should praise Him because His Word says He always provides an answer, or the way out of a situation (1 Cor. 10:13). When we can quiet our souls and begin to praise Him for the chance to allow His power and glory to be reflected in our lives, then we will get answers for our problems. We are not praising Him for the problem but rather praising Him in spite of the problem. We must not allow the enemy to rob us of our joy because of the problem.

If a Christian discerns that something in his life is from the enemy, he should <u>resist</u> that, using the Sword of the Spirit as an offensive weapon (**Eph. 6:17-18**) along with the keys which we are discussing in this workbook.

Romans 8:28 is often misquoted and misconstrued. That verse does not say that everything always works for the good of everyone. In the first place it defines those for whom all things <u>do</u> work together for good as: those who love God and are called according to his purpose.

God can take what the devil meant for evil and bring good out of it, as long as our attitudes remain right.

David wrote in several psalms that we should let God's praise be <u>continually</u> (constantly or always) in our mouths (**Pss. 34:1, 40:3, 75:1,** and others).

God said that **Whoso offereth praise glorifieth me** (**Ps. 50:23**).

Praise also is a great weapon against the devil. Verses such as **Psalm 34:1-4** can be used as patterns for praising God in times of attack by the enemy. In fact, that entire psalm is a good one to quote against the enemy and to remember that we are to fear (reverence) God and not Satan if we want deliverance. Praise delivers us from fear.

Christ Unlimited — P.O. Box 850 — Dewey, AZ 86327   USA

Other Aspects of Praise

Other ways in which <u>praise</u> is a key to the Kingdom are:

*Praise brings God's healing, kindness, mercy, plenty, restoration of youth and strength, righteous judgment, and deliverance from oppression (Pss. 34, 103).

*Praise can deliver us from depression. Being depressed or oppressed is like being in a "pit," and David said praise is the way out of a pit (Ps. 30:1-4).

In the New Testament, **Philippians 4:4-8** tells us praise will deliver us from worry and anxiety, both of which are sinful.

Rejoice in the Lord alway: and again I say, Rejoice. Let your moderation be known unto all men. The Lord is at hand. Be careful (do not worry) for nothing; but in every thing by prayer and supplication with thanksgiving let your requests be made known unto God. And the peace of God, which passeth all understanding, shall keep your hearts and minds through Christ Jesus. Finally, brethren, whatsoever things are true, whatsoever things are honest, whatsoever things are just, whatsoever things are pure, whatsoever things are lovely, whatsoever things are of good report; if there be any virtue, and if there be any praise, think on these things.

Anyone who slips into the subtle sins of worry and anxiety needs to repent and begin to operate in the remedy for these attitudes,

Christ Unlimited — P.O. Box 850 — Dewey, AZ 86327   USA

which is to think on true, pure, and good things, according to the Word of God (Phil. 4:8).

*Praise can win our battles, with the classic example being in the battle of the Israelites against a natural enemy where the Lord won the battle for them as soon as they began to sing and praise God.

And when he had consulted with the people, he appointed singers unto the Lord, and that should praise the beauty of holiness, as they went out before the army, and to say, Praise the Lord; for his mercy endureth for ever. And when they began to sing and to praise, the Lord set ambushments against the children of Ammon, Moab, and mount Seir, which were come against Judah; and they were smitten. For the children of Ammon and Moab stood up against the inhabitants of mount Seir, utterly to slay and destroy them: and when they had made an end of the inhabitants of Seir, every one helped to destroy another. And when Judah came toward the watch tower in the wilderness, they looked unto the multitude, and, behold, they were dead bodies fallen to the earth, and none escaped.

2 Chronicles 20:21-24

David knew that he could not deal with Goliath, but he also knew beyond a shadow of a doubt that God could, through him. And he also knew that God would. Even as a youth, David had spent much time praising God, so He knew God's ways.

*Praise can open prison doors, as Paul and Silas found out (Acts 16:25,26). "Prison" for us may mean emotional, physical, or mental bondage. One way out is to praise God. **Psalm 22:3** says, But thou art holy, O thou that inhabitest the praises of Israel.

The next three <u>keys</u> are related but involve different ways or attitudes of prayer — general kinds of prayer, intercession, and travail.

The Third Key: Prayer

There are various ways of praying, some right and some wrong or ineffective. For example, people get concerned about body postures while praying and forget that attitudes of the heart are more important.

In the Bible, we see examples of many different postures in prayer, all of which are fine. We can lift our hands (**Ps. 63:4; 1 Tim. 2:8**), which symbolizes surrender and a willingness to receive. We can bow our heads (**Gen. 24:26; Neh. 8:6**); we can kneel (**Acts 20:36**); we can lie on our faces (**Matt. 26:39**); and we can look upward toward Heaven (**1 Kings 8:22**).

The proper way to begin our prayers is by addressing the Father in the name of Jesus. We should pray to the Father through the name of Jesus (**John 16:23**), just as we cast out demons in the name of Jesus, not in another name (**Mark 16:17,18**). In other words, our "door" to the Father is Jesus, and the authority in which we operate lies in His blood having covered our sins and in His name as Conquering King.

There <u>are</u> two extremes to avoid in seeking God for the things we desire: (1) constantly asking Him over and over for the same thing or (2) avoiding praying about something for fear of "bothering" Him.

Yes, we are to "seek, ask, and knock" (**Matt. 7:7,8**) and keep on doing this. But first, we should find God's will concerning the matters about which we are praying, either through His Word or through a witness from the Holy Spirit.

At some point in prayer, a breakthrough should be felt in the spirit; and, after that, we can simply thank God for the manifestation of the answer until it comes.

We should persist until we have the witness that the matter has been taken care of, which usually is before we see the answer. We are to "walk by faith and not by sight" (**2 Cor. 5:7**). However, if we keep on and on at God about something that is not His best for us, He may reluctantly give us that thing. The results will not be God's best for us.

They soon forgat his works; they waited not for his counsel: But lusted exceedingly in the wilderness, and tempted God in the desert. And he gave them their request; but sent leanness into their soul.

Psalm 106:13-15

The right way to find out God's will is through study of the Word and through prayer. The wrong way is through experiencing the consequences of disobedience by not consulting Him and making decisions out of His will.

Continuing to beg God for something over and over is not acting in faith as at some point in our making of requests, we must believe that we receive the thing we ask for before we see it with our natural eyes.

Therefore I say unto you, What things soever ye desire, when ye pray, believe that ye receive them, and ye shall have them.

Mark 11:24

On the other hand, we should not hesitate to pray about something for fear of bothering God. He is concerned over even the smallest details of our lives as we are told that even the hairs on our heads are numbered (Matt. 10:30).

Since the Lord says to seek Him in prayer about our needs and desires, to avoid repetition about a certain need I will pray different ways about the problem. I then daily thank Him for the answer that I believe He is sending. Sometimes I receive answers quickly, at other times it may take years, especially when other people's wills are involved.

I (Betty) prayed for my father's salvation for more than 20 years, and God is faithful as I was able to lead my father to the Lord after I had grown up and married.

Another way to pray is the prayer of agreement.

Again I say unto you, That if two of you shall agree on earth as touching any thing that they shall ask, it shall be done for them

Christ Unlimited — P.O. Box 850 — Dewey, AZ 86327   USA

of my Father which is in heaven.

Matthew 18:19

Again, this is based on the request being in God's will. If someone asks us to agree with them on an unspoken request, we can agree for God's will to be done in that situation, but we cannot agree with the request without knowing what it is. If we are asking others to be in agreement, we should choose those who have great faith as well as understanding of how God works.

The Bible also speaks about certain methods employed along with our prayers. These are:

*Praying while anointing with oil (James 5:14,15)

*Prayer that accompanies the laying on of hands (Matt. 19:13; Acts 8:18-20; Heb. 6:2).

*Speaking forth scriptures from the Word of God as prayers (Matt. 8:8), which can be speaking His word over someone else or standing on promises from the Bible for ourselves.

Answers seem to come more quickly when we pray <u>fervent and diligent</u> prayers (James 5:16). That is especially true when we are praying the prayer of intercession.

The Fourth Key: Intercessory Prayer

The prayer of intercession is prayed for someone else, not for ourselves. Jesus is our pattern in this, as well as in all else. He is our Mediator, our Intercessor before the Father (Isa. 53:12; Heb. 7:25), the greatest intercessor of all time. God still seeks

Christ Unlimited — P.O. Box 850 — Dewey, AZ 86327   USA

intercessors today so that judgment can be averted and sinners saved.

> And I sought for a man among them, that should make up the hedge, and stand in the gap before me for the land, that I should not destroy it: but I found none. Therefore have I poured out mine indignation upon them; I have consumed them with the fire of my wrath: their own way have I recompensed upon their heads, saith the Lord God.
>
> Ezekiel 22:30,31

An example of this is how Abraham interceded for the cities of Sodom and Gomorrah to be spared destruction (Gen.18:17-33), although Lot and his two daughters were all that escaped. The first ministry that believers are called to is the "ministry of reconciliation and intercession." The purpose of this kind of intercession is for the Father to draw people unto Jesus through the Holy Spirit.

> And all things are of God, who hath reconciled us to himself by Jesus Christ, and hath given to us the ministry of reconciliation; To wit, that God was in Christ, reconciling the world unto himself, not imputing their trespasses unto them; and hath committed unto us the word of reconciliation.
>
> 2 Cor. 5:18-20

No man can come to me, except the Father which hath sent me

draw him: and I will raise him up at the last day.

John 6:44

Christians should offer many prayers directed to the salvation of others (John 17:20; Luke 9:53-56). We are to also especially pray for those in authority.

I exhort therefore, that, first of all, supplications, prayers, intercessions, and giving of thanks, be made for all men; For kings, and for all that are in authority; that we may lead a quiet and peaceable life in all godliness and honesty. For this is good and acceptable in the sight of God our Saviour; Who will have all men to be saved, and to come unto the knowledge of the truth. For there is one God, and one mediator between God and men, the man Christ Jesus; Who gave himself a ransom for all, to be testified in due time.

1 Timothy 2:1-6

That means praying for our pastors and for civil authorities — locally, nationally, and worldwide.

People called into the specific ministry of intercession will many times feel the infirmities of the people for whom they pray (Heb. 4:15). They may sense fear or oppression on those for whom they are interceding, and when this "lifts," they know the person is free. They can stop praying about that particular situation then.

Christ Unlimited — P.O. Box 850 — Dewey, AZ 86327   USA

The Fifth Key: Travailing Prayer

Travailing Prayer is one of crying out or groaning in the spirit. John 16:20,22 tells us that travail is an agony or anguish of heart and is really the manifestation of the grief of the heart of God.

Verily, verily, I say unto you, That ye shall weep and lament, but the world shall rejoice: and ye shall be sorrowful, but your sorrow shall be turned into joy. . . . And ye now therefore have sorrow, but I will see you again, and your heart shall rejoice, and your joy no man taketh from you.

John 16:20,22

Travailing prayer cries out in tears to God. It is the Holy Spirit using our <u>hearts</u> and our emotions to cry in sorrow for others, to grieve over things that grieve Him, and also to minister to other people.

Jesus travailed when Lazarus was raised from the dead (John 11:33) and in the Garden of Gethsemane, when He prayed through in order to be able to endure the events of the next day in peace and authority. His perspiration was as "great drops of blood" because of the agony of soul manifested in travail (Luke 22:44).

We often feel sorrow in this world, but this kind is fleshly sorrow. Many times it stems from self-pity or self-centeredness. Even grief over the death of a loved one becomes "flesh" and a sin if it causes one's life to stop at that point. Godly sorrow means taking on burdens in the spirit for other people.

Christ Unlimited — P.O. Box 850 — Dewey, AZ 86327   USA

For godly sorrow worketh repentance to salvation not to be repented of, but the sorrow of the world worketh death.

2 Corinthians 7:10

Many times when we cry over situations, things are released in the spiritual realm for God to operate more quickly. Travailing prayer breaks things more quickly than any other kind of prayer or any other key. The psalmist wrote that the kind of grieving or travailing that God does through us will produce joy in the end.

They that sow in tears shall reap in joy. He that goeth forth and weepeth, bearing precious seed, shall doubtless come again with rejoicing, bringing his sheaves with him.

Psalm 126:5,6

Romans 8:26,27 says that travailing can be groanings too deep for words, for the Holy Spirit sometimes makes intercession for us that way. Travail can be for the purpose of cleansing ourselves from weaknesses or infirmities, or it can be for other people. Praying in tongues with tears can be a cleansing from sin.

Travailing prayer needs to be undertaken with wisdom. It is likened to a woman giving birth, so it should not be done in public under ordinary circumstances. Men, as well as women, may feel pains similar to birth pains while travailing. Jeremiah spoke about men having "birth pains" (Jer. 30:5,6).

There might be such a time of travail come upon someone in a prayer meeting or special meeting, but this kind of prayer is not something a person simply decides to do. This kind of prayer is undertaken under the leading of, or a burden from, the Holy Spirit. Another exception is when the Spirit of God falls on an entire congregation to corporately travail for the birth of something He wants accomplished.

A person cannot simply decide to travail; however, many times fervent and diligent praying over a person or situation will lead into times of travailing. The purposes of travail are to produce spiritual children, to birth things in the spiritual realm that will later manifest in the natural, to meet urgent financial needs, or for the manifestation of healings. Paul wrote to the Christians at Galatia that he was travailing for Christ to be formed in them.

> My little children, of whom I travail in birth again until Christ be formed in you.
>
> Galatians 4:19

Travailing affects the physical body. Daniel wrote that he travailed or was grieved in his body (**Dan. 7:15**). Travail begins in the spirit and then is reflected in the body. Daniel also fainted while in travail and felt sick after several days (**Dan. 8:27**). Again, he wrote that he felt weak and retained no strength (**Dan. 10:8**). Weeping, sorrow, and bitterness of soul also are forms of travail, as Hannah experienced while praying for a son, Samuel (**1 Sam. 1:10**).

The Sixth Key to the Kingdom: Fasting

Fasting is the offering up of the body as a sacrifice through the abstinence from food. This is not the same as dieting to lose weight, although fasting does have a benefit to the body through the automatic cleansing of toxins during the fast. There are several different ways of fasting. The most common is the way Jesus fasted — no food, but he drank water (Luke 4). Paul did a three-day absolute fast at least once (Acts 9:9), but this was a supernatural result of his conversion on the road to Damascus.

Moses also apparently spent 40 days on Mt. Sinai without food or water, but again, he spent that time in the presence of God (Ex. 24:18). Paul and Moses's fasts were divinely appointed. Going without water is not advisable for the average person to try. Under normal circumstances, the physical body cannot exist without water for very long.

Another type of fast is a partial fast. Daniel fasted all "pleasant" food for three weeks (Dan. 10:3), and some Christians today fast solid foods but drink liquids. This is particularly advisable if a person must continue to do physical labor while fasting. Not eating meat, or desserts, or some other particular food for a period of time could also be a partial fast. If the heart is right, God will honor any kind of fast.

However, if a person fasts for the wrong reasons, the fast will not do any good. For example, fasting is not attempting to get God to do something. Fasting afflicts the soul (Isa. 58:5) — the mind, will, and emotions — as well as the body and moves the person to a place of being able to pray through or to a place where intense spiritual warfare can be waged. Fasting also can move the devil out of the way. Because Jesus had just fasted 40 days, He was quick to defeat the devil (Matt. 4:1-4). Fasting "looses" the bonds of wickedness (Isa. 58:6). Therefore, fasting does not move God's hand, but rather makes Satan turn loose of what he is holding back from us.

Fasting is not to be done to be seen of man (Matt. 6:16-18). That motive totally ruins the effect of the fast. We are to "fast unto the Lord." The length of a fast will vary as the Lord leads, and anything over seven days certainly should have the mandate of the Lord. Some people fasting legalistically and not under the Holy Spirit have damaged their bodies.

In Isaiah 58:6,7, the Lord said that fasting will release us to be able to look after the hungry and the homeless and see them set free. Fasting can be: ...not doing thine own ways, nor finding thine own pleasure, nor speaking thine own words, according to Isaiah 58:13, the fasting chapter. That chapter also lays down guidelines for keeping the Sabbath, a form of "fasting" work and business for one day a week (vs. 13,14).

Other reasons for fasting include:

*Building faith (Matt. 17:21)

*To make it easier to hear God (Acts 13:2,3)

*To bring the flesh into subjection to the spirit (Matt. 4:1-4)

*To minister to the Lord (Acts 13:2)

*To speed up answers to prayer (Isa. 58:8,9)

*To release blessings (Isa. 58:10-12)

Christ Unlimited — P.O. Box 850 — Dewey, AZ 86327   USA

Overcoming Life Memory Verse

The suggested memory verse for Section Two is:

Is not this the fast that I have chosen? to loose the bands of wickedness, to undo the heavy burdens, and to let the oppressed go free, and that ye break every yoke?

Isaiah 58:6

Christ Unlimited — P.O. Box 850 — Dewey, AZ 86327   USA

Lesson for Section Two

I. Praise and Worship

A. Is praise and worship limited to singing?

_____

1. Did Jesus praise the Father?

_____

...Our Father which art in heaven, <u>Hallowed</u> be thy name. Thy
kingdom come. Thy will be done, as in heaven, so in earth.

Luke 11:2

2. There are praises in _____.
   Reference: Revelation 19:5-7

3. The Bible tells us to be joyful, praise God, and give thanks
   in _____, no matter what the conditions
   or circumstances are that surround us.

Rejoice evermore. Pray without ceasing. In every thing give
thanks: for this is the will of God in Christ Jesus concerning you.

1 Thessalonians 5:16-18

a. That means it is God's will for us to _____
   in everything. It does not mean everything we experience

Christ Unlimited — P.O. Box 850 — Dewey, AZ 86327   USA

is God's will for us; otherwise, there would be no need for discernment or resisting certain things.

b. Things work together for good to those who are _____ according to His purpose (Rom. 8:28).

B. _____ and _____ will unlock the Kingdom of God to us.

1. Praise is a weapon against the devil and can deliver us from the following things: (Use the scripture references below to identify them)

a. _____

b. _____

c. _____

References:

I sought the Lord, and he heard me, and delivered me from all my fears.

Psalm 34:4

Rejoice in the Lord alway: and again I say, Rejoice. Let your moderation be known unto all men. The Lord is at hand. <u>Be careful for nothing</u>; but in everything by prayer and supplication with thanksgiving let your requests be made known unto God.

Philippians 4:4-6

I will extol thee, O Lord; for thou hast lifted me up, and hast not made my foes to rejoice over me. O Lord my God, I cried unto thee, and thou hast healed me. O Lord, thou hast brought up my soul from the grave: thou hast kept me alive, that I should not go down to the pit. Sing unto the Lord, O ye saints of his, and give thanks at the remembrance of his holiness.

Psalm 30:1-4

2. Praise brings:

a. God's healing, kindness, mercy, plenty, youth, strength, and _____ from oppression

b. _____ judgment on our behalf.

Bless the Lord, O my soul: and all that is within me, bless his holy name. Bless the Lord, O my soul, and forget not all his benefits: Who forgiveth all thine iniquities; who healeth all thy diseases; who redeemeth thy life from destruction; who crowneth thee with lovingkindness and tender mercies; Who satisfieth thy mouth with good things; so that thy youth is renewed like the eagle's. The Lord executeth <u>righteousness</u> and <u>judgment </u>for all that are oppressed.

Psalm 103:1-6

3. Praise can win our _____.

And he said, Hearken ye, all Judah, and ye inhabitants of Jerusalem, and thou king Jehoshaphat. Thus saith the Lord unto you, Be not afraid nor dismayed by reason of this great multitude; <u>for the battle is not yours</u>, but God's. ...And when he had consulted with the people, he appointed singers unto the Lord, and that should praise the beauty of holiness, as they went out before the army, and to say, Praise the Lord; for his mercy endureth for ever. And when they began to sing and to praise, the Lord set ambushments against the children of Ammon, Moab, and mount Seir, which were come against Judah; and they were smitten.

2 Chronicles 20:15,21,22

4. The Holy Spirit _____ our praises.

But thou art holy, O thou that inhabitest the praises of Israel.

Psalm 22:3

5. Praise opens _____ doors (Acts 16:25,26).

And at midnight Paul and Silas prayed, and sang praises unto God: and the prisoners heard them. And suddenly there was a great earthquake, so that the foundations of the prison were shaken: and immediately all the doors were opened, and every one's bands were loosed.

II. Prayer

A. Answers to prayer only come if we pray according to the principles in God's Word. What are some of these principles?

1. We must ask according to God's _____

Christ Unlimited — P.O. Box 850 — Dewey, AZ 86327   USA

And this is the confidence that we have in him, that, if we ask any thing according to his will he heareth us: And if we know that he hear us, whatsoever we ask, we know that we have the petitions that we desired of him.

1 John 5:14,15

2. We must have our own wills _____ to God.

I can of mine own self do nothing: as I hear, I judge: and my judgment is just; because I seek not mine own will, but the will of the Father which hath sent me. . . . If ye abide in me, and my words abide in you, ye shall ask what ye will, and it shall be done unto you.

John 5:30, 15:7

3. We must ask with the proper _____ and _____.

Ye ask, and receive not, because ye ask amiss, that ye may consume it upon your lusts.

James 4:3

B. Two extremes to avoid when desiring things of God are:

  1. _____

  2. _____

They soon forgat his works; they waited not for his counsel: But lusted exceedingly in the wilderness, and tempted God in the desert. And he gave them their request; but sent leanness into their soul.

Psalm 106:13-15

C. Is there any one "correct" posture to assume when praying? _____. Some ways to pray or worship include:

   1. _____ up our hands

I will therefore that men pray every where lifting up holy hands, without wrath and doubting.

1 Timothy 2:8

Thus will I bless thee while I live: I will lift up my hands in thy name.

Psalm 63:4

   a. Lifting up hands symbolizes _____ and a willingness to receive.

   b. Lifted hands also means the person has a _____ to be noticed, or is attempting to attract someone's attention — in prayer, the Lord's attention.

   2. _____ our heads

And the man bowed down his head, and worshipped the Lord.

Genesis 24:26

Christ Unlimited — P.O. Box 850 — Dewey, AZ 86327   USA

And Ezra blessed the Lord, the great God. And all the people answered, Amen, Amen, with lifting up their hands: and they bowed their heads, and worshipped the Lord with their faces to the ground.

> Nehemiah 8:6

3. _____ down

And when he had thus spoken, he kneeled down, and prayed with them all.

> Acts 20:36

4. _____ on our faces

And he went a little further, and fell on his face, and prayed, saying, O my Father, if it be possible, let this cup pass from me: nevertheless not as I will, but as thou wilt.

> Matthew 26:39

5. With hands and faces turned toward_____

And Solomon stood before the altar of the Lord in the presence of all the congregation of Israel, and spread forth his hands toward heaven.

> 1 Kings 8:22

Christ Unlimited — P.O. Box 850 — Dewey, AZ 86327   USA

6. What is more important in prayer than any particular posture or position?

_____

Reference: Luke 18:10-14

D. List some different methods of prayer in the Bible:

1. _____ with oil

Is any sick among you? let him call for the elders of the church; and let them pray over him, anointing him with oil in the name of the Lord: And the prayer of faith shall save the sick, and the Lord shall raise him up; and if he have committed sins, they shall be forgiven him.

James 5:14,15

2. _____ of hands

Then were there brought unto him little children, that he should put his hands on them, and pray . . . .

Matthew 19:13

And when Simon saw that through laying on of the apostles' hands the Holy Ghost was given, he offered them money, Saying, Give me also this power, that on whomsoever I lay hands, he may receive the Holy Ghost. But Peter said unto him,

Christ Unlimited — P.O. Box 850 — Dewey, AZ 86327   USA

Thy money perish with thee, because thou hast thought that the gift of God may be purchased with money.

Acts 8:18-20

Of the doctrine of baptisms, and of laying on of hands, and of resurrection of the dead, and of eternal judgment.

Hebrews 6:2

  3. _____ the Word in faith

The centurion answered and said, Lord, I am not worthy that thou shouldest come under my roof: but speak the word only, and my servant shall be healed.

Matthew 8:8

  4. The prayer of _____

Verily I say unto you, Whatsoever ye shall bind on earth shall be bound in heaven: and whatsoever ye shall loose on earth shall be loosed in heaven. Again I say unto you, That if two of you shall agree on earth as touching any thing that they shall ask, it shall be done for them of my Father which is in heaven.

Matthew 18:18,19

  5. Speaking in the _____ of Jesus

And in that day ye shall ask me nothing. Verily, verily, I say unto you, Whatsoever ye shall ask the Father in my name, he will give it you.

John 16:23

And these signs shall follow them that believe; In my name shall they cast out devils; they shall speak with new tongues; They shall take up serpents; and if they drink any deadly thing, it shall not hurt them; they shall lay hands on the sick, and they shall recover.

Mark 16:17,18

6. _____ and diligent prayer

Ask, and it shall be given you; seek, and ye shall find; knock, and it shall be opened unto you: For every one that asketh receiveth; and he that seeketh findeth; and to him that knocketh it shall be opened.

Matthew 7:7,8

Confess your faults one to another, and pray one for another, that ye may be healed. The effectual fervent prayer of a righteous man availeth much.

James 5:16

Pray without ceasing.

1 Thessalonians 5:17

Christ Unlimited — P.O. Box 850 — Dewey, AZ 86327   USA

7. Praying the _____ Prayer

    Reference: Matthew 6:5-13

III. Intercessory Prayer

A. What is intercessory prayer?

_____

    References: Isaiah 53:12; 1 Timothy 2:1-4; Hebrews 7:25

1. Who is the greatest intercessor of all time? _____

2. Is God still seeking intercessors today? _____
For what two reasons?

    a. To avert _____

    b. To save _____

And I sought for a man among them, that should make up the hedge, and stand in the gap before me for the land, that I should not destroy it: but I found none. Therefore have I poured out mine indignation upon them; I have consumed them with the fire of my wrath: their own way have I recompensed upon their heads, saith thy Lord God.

                             Ezekiel 22:30,31

B. The ministry of intercession involves _____
to the Holy Spirit.

Christ Unlimited — P.O. Box 850 — Dewey, AZ 86327   USA

Likewise the Spirit also helpeth our infirmities: for we know not what we should pray for as we ought; but the Spirit itself maketh intercession for us with groanings which cannot be uttered. And he that searcheth the hearts knoweth what is the mind of the Spirit, because he maketh intercession for the saints according to the will of God.

Romans 8:26,27

C. The first ministry believers are called to fill is that of:

_____ and _____.

And all things are of God, who hath reconciled us to himself by Jesus Christ, and hath given to us the ministry of reconciliation; To wit, that God was in Christ, reconciling the world unto himself, not imputing their trespasses unto them; and hath committed unto us the word of reconciliation. Now then we are ambassadors for Christ, as though God did beseech you by us: we pray you in Christ's stead, be ye reconciled to God.

2 Corinthians 5:18-20

1. The ministry of intercession is to enable the Holy Spirit to _____ people unto Himself.

No man can come to me, except the Father which hath sent me draw him: and I will raise him up at the last day.

John 6:44

Christ Unlimited — P.O. Box 850 — Dewey, AZ 86327   USA

2. We also are told in the Bible to intercede for those in

_____.

   Reference: 1 Timothy 2:1-6

IV. Travailing Prayer

   A. What is travailing prayer?

   _____

   _____

Verily, verily I say unto you, That ye shall weep and lament, but the world shall rejoice: and ye shall be sorrowful, but your sorrow shall be turned into joy. A woman when she is in travail hath sorrow, because her hour is come: but as soon as she is delivered of the child, she remembereth no more the anguish, for joy that a man is born into the world. And ye now therefore have sorrow: but I will see you again, and your heart shall rejoice, and your joy no man taketh from you.

                                                    John 16:20-22

B. In travailing prayer, God uses our _____ and _____ to weep and cry through. The Spirit of God expresses sorrow in this manner for others.

Rejoice with them that do rejoice, and weep with them that weep.

                                                    Romans 12:15

Christ Unlimited — P.O. Box 850 — Dewey, AZ 86327   USA

1. Crying in the Spirit brings life and _____ after it is finished.

They that sow in tears shall reap in joy. He that goeth forth and weepeth, bearing precious seed, shall doubtless come again with rejoicing, bringing his sheaves with him.

Psalm 126:5,6

2. What are two kinds of sorrow about which Paul wrote to the Corinthians?

a. _____ sorrow

b. _____ sorrow

For godly sorrow worketh repentance to salvation not to be repented of: but the sorrow of the world worketh death.

2 Corinthians 7:10

C. Sometimes the spirit of travail occurs deep within us and the tears or cries cannot be _____.

Likewise the Spirit also helpeth our infirmities: for we know not what we should pray for as we ought: but the Spirit itself maketh intercession for us with groanings which cannot be uttered.

Romans 8:26

Christ Unlimited — P.O. Box 850 — Dewey, AZ 86327   USA

1. This kind of prayer can be for the _____
   of our own infirmities and weaknesses.

2. Also, it can be on the behalf of _____.

D. Name three purposes of travail according to the scripture
   reference's below:

1. _____

2. _____

3. _____

. . . for as soon as Zion travailed, she brought forth her children.

Isaiah 66:8

Who now rejoice in my sufferings for you, and fill up that which
is behind of the afflictions of Christ in my flesh for his body's
sake, which is the church.

Colossians 1:24

My little children, of whom I travail in birth again until Christ be
formed in you.

Galatians 4:19

E. What are four different ways in which travail is manifested?

1. _____

I Daniel <u>grieved</u> in my spirit in the midst of my body, and the visions in my head troubled me.

Daniel 7:15

2. Feeling _____

And I Daniel fainted, and was sick certain days; afterward I rose up, and did the king's business: and I was astonished at the vision, but none understood it.... Therefore I was left alone, and saw this great vision, and there remained no strength in me: for my comeliness was turned in me into corruption, and I retained no strength.

Daniel 8:27, 10:8

3. Weeping, sorrow, and _____

References: 1 Samuel 1:13,15

And she was in bitterness of soul, and prayed unto the Lord and wept sore.

1 Samuel 1:10

4. _____ pains

For thus saith the Lord; We have heard a voice of trembling, of fear, and not of peace. Ask ye now, and see whether a man

Christ Unlimited — P.O. Box 850 — Dewey, AZ 86327   USA

doth travail with child? Wherefore do I see every man with his hands on his loins, as a woman in travail, and all faces are turned into paleness?

Jeremiah 30:5,6

F. Did Jesus travail while on earth? _____

   1. He groaned in the spirit when _____ was being raised from the dead.
   Reference: John 11:32-44

   2. The greatest travail of all time was the Lord's travail in the

   _____.

   Reference: Luke 22:41-44

G. There is a right _____ and place for travail.

A time to weep, and a time to laugh; a time to mourn, and a time to dance.

Ecclesiastes 3:4

   1. Should travail usually be done publicly or privately?

   _____

   2. Why? _____

   _____

V. Fasting

A. What is fasting?

_____

_____

Is it such a fast that I have chosen? a day for a man to afflict his soul? . . .

Isaiah 58:5

1. Fasting is to produce _____ results, such as cleansing and having spiritual "eyes" opened (Acts 9:9-19).

2. Fasting is unto the _____, not to be seen of men (Matt. 6:16-18).

3. Fasting also brings the _____ into subjection to the Holy Spirit (Matt. 4:1-4)

4. Fasting also is a form of mourning and suffering for Christ, and a way of _____ unto the Lord (Ezra 10:6; Neh. 1:4; Acts 13:2).

B. Fasting also can be a _____ _____ effort.

Sanctify ye a fast, call a solemn assembly, gather the elders and all the inhabitants of the land into the house of the Lord your God, and cry unto the Lord.

Joel 1:14

Christ Unlimited — P.O. Box 850 — Dewey, AZ 86327   USA

C. Jesus fasted _____, but drank water (Luke 4).

List some different kinds of fasts:

1. _____

2. _____

And he (Paul) was three days without sight, and neither did he eat nor drink.

Acts 9:9

[The Apostle Paul fasted often — 2 Cor. 11:27.]

3. _____

I ate no pleasant bread, neither came flesh nor wine in my mouth, neither did I anoint myself at all, till three whole weeks were fulfilled.

Daniel 10:3

4. Which kind is considered the "normal," most common, way to fast? _____

D. How should we decide which kind of fast and for how long it should last? _____

E. One particular chapter in the Bible deals the most with this subject and is called the _____ chapter.

Christ Unlimited — P.O. Box 850 — Dewey, AZ 86327   USA

1. Which chapter is this? _____

2. We find in **Isaiah 58** some benefits and purposes of fasting. List three of these:

   a. _____

   b. _____

   c. _____

F. Fasting can build _____.

   Reference: **Matthew 17:21**

G. Fasting also can give us _____ over Satan.

   Reference: **Matthew 4:1-11**

Christ Unlimited — P.O. Box 850 — Dewey, AZ 86327   USA

Overcoming Life Memory Verse

The suggested memory verse for this section is:

And I will give unto thee the keys of the kingdom of heaven: and whatsoever thou shalt bind on earth shall be bound in heaven: and whatsoever thou shalt loose on earth shall be loosed in heaven.

Matthew 16:19

Review Outline, Section Two

I. Prayer

A. Communicating with God

1. Asking, desiring, requesting

   a. Petitions must agree with the Word (1 John 5:14,15).

   b. A Christian must ask in humility and dependence on God.

   c. We must never demand anything of God in rebellion.

   d. We also must avoid a sense of unworthiness.

2. The Lord's will regarding prayer:

   a. He wants us to ask (Matt. 7:7)

   b. He wants to answer.

   c. He withholds only for our good.

   d. He promises to care for our basic needs.

   e. He gives us blessings when we can handle them.

3. Dangers of "demanding," lustful prayers are: (Ps. 106: 13-15)

   a. God answers them reluctantly by allowing us to reap what we sow.

   b. They open the door to Satan's answers.

   c. They result in "leanness of soul."

   d. They cause a loss of joy and love in serving Jesus.

4. Forms and Methods of Prayer

   a. Attitude is more important than posture or form.

   b. The prayer of agreement (Matt. 18:18,19) has "rules."

      1) It must be based on the Word of God

      2) It must agree with the Holy Spirit.

Christ Unlimited — P.O. Box 850 — Dewey, AZ 86327   USA

          3) It can be tested by the principle of two or three witnesses (Matt. 18:16).

          4) We bind or loose what has been bound or loosed in Heaven.

     c. Praying in tongues, or praying in the Spirit (1 Cor.14:14, 15: see section one of this workbook.)

          1) Praying to God, not man

          2) Hinders Satan: He cannot understand the prayer

          3) An important part of prayer life and the Great Commission (Mark 16:15-18); edifies the Spirit

          4) Two types: a prayer language and a ministry gift to the body that must be interpreted

  5. Basic principles of prayer:

     a. Prayers are to the Father in Jesus' name (John 16:23).

     b. Pray without ceasing (1 Thess. 5:17).

     c. Prayer may not be answered immediately, so:

          1) Do not get discouraged.

          2) Focus on God, not problems.

     d. "Pray through" until peace comes.

     e. Pray in one's native tongue and in "tongues."

     f. Forgive others in order to obtain victory in prayer.

     g. Use the Lord's Prayer as an example (Matt. 6:9-13).

II. Other Keys to the Kingdom

  A. Praise: the will of God

    1. We are to praise Him: (1 Thess. 5:16,18; Rev. 19:5-7).

      a. Continually

Christ Unlimited — P.O. Box 850 — Dewey, AZ 86327   USA

b. In the midst of trials as well as blessings

2. Praise can be offered as a sacrifice (Jer. 33:11).

3. Praise brings healing and deliverance (Ps. 30:1-4; 42:11).

B. Intercession

1. Intercession is praying for others (1 Tim. 2:1-6).

2. Jesus is the greatest intercessor of all time (Heb. 7:25).

3. God seeks those "to stand in the gap" (Ezek. 22:30-31).

C. Travail

1. A manifestation of God's heart (John 16:20-22) in crying, moaning, or groaning (as Jesus did in Luke 22:44).

2. Begins with a burden or unction from the Holy Spirit; is not self-induced.

3. Begins with grief, ends with joy.

4. Produces a birthing in the spiritual realm of new converts, matured saints, or ministries that God wants accomplished.

5. A form of suffering for Christ; forms the image of Christ in believers.

6. Ranges from a mild heaviness or depression to deep groan and birthlike labor pains in men as well as in women.

7. Breaks yokes of bondage, brings the Kingdom of God to earth.

D. Fasting

1. A normal fast is to drink water, but eat no food.

2. Fasting should be under the guidance of the Holy Spirit.

3. Fasting is primarily for spiritual purposes.

4. Fasting is to:

    a. Loose the bands of wickedness (Isa. 58:6).

    b. Accomplish spiritual cleansing.

    c. Make a person more sensitive to the Lord's voice.

    d. Help in traviling prayer (Ezra 10:6; Neh. 1:4) and to speed up answers.

    e. Bring the flesh under authority of the spirit.

    f. Minister unto the Lord (Acts 13:2).

5. Fasting changes us and moves the devil out of the way; it is not to move God as He already has done His part.

6. Prerequisites for effective fasting are humility before God and love and mercy towards others.

7. Fruits of fasting included healing, spiritual strength, restoration spiritually, physically, and materially.

8. God's ultimate desire is for us to be overcomers, which means living a "fasted life" in all areas.

Christ Unlimited — P.O. Box 850 — Dewey, AZ 86327   USA

Review Outline Quiz, Section Two

1. What is prayer?

   _____

2. When are we to praise the Lord?

   _____

3. Intercession is for what purpose?

   _____

4. Travail is a deeper level of prayer and intercession that often manifests in loud _____, _____, or _____.

5. Travail begins with _____, but ends with _____.

6. Praise and worship is defined only as singing to God.

   True _____ False _____

7. Fasting is primarily for _____ purposes.

8. A _____ fast is to go without food but drink water.

9. Fasting looses the _____ of wickedness.

10. What kind of life is God's ultimate desire for us?

   _____

Christ Unlimited — P.O. Box 850 — Dewey, AZ 86327   USA

What You Need to Know About
Christ Unlimited Ministries

Purpose and Vision

Go ye therefore, and teach all nations, baptizing them in the name of the Father, and of the Son, and of the Holy Ghost: Teaching them to observe all things whatsoever I have commanded you: and, lo, I am with you always, even unto the end of the world. Amen.

Matthew 28:19, 20

CHRIST UNLIMITED is not "another denomination," sect, or just a separate group. It is an arm of the Body of Christ — the Church of Jesus Christ, which has been called to strengthen the Body at large. We also believe we have been called to help establish the Kingdom of God in the earth.

CHRIST UNLIMITED is open to help and work with all Bible-believing Christians regardless of their church or denominational affiliations and committed to helping wherever possible in evangelistic and teaching outreaches.

CHRIST UNLIMITED believes that time is running out and the Gospel has not been preached to every creature. Many nations have not heard the Gospel, and in many places, doors for evangelism are closing. We believe it is time all Christians cooperated with the Lord in breaking down denominational walls for a united front line against the kingdom of darkness and in setting up the Kingdom of the Lord Jesus Christ by the power of the Holy Spirit.

CHRIST UNLIMITED provides such tools as to enable the saints of God to establish the Kingdom of God in the earth. We encourage groups of prayer warriors who will pray, fast, and intercede for the nations. This, we believe, is weapon number one. We teach believers how to overcome through spiritual warfare and through knowing how to use their authority in Christ Jesus through the Word and the power of the Holy Spirit.

Christians need to know how to bring down the forces of darkness in their own lives and in the lives of those to whom they minister. We provide such tools as Bibles, literature, **CHRIST UNLIMITED** books, and downloadable audio and video. We promote the Gospel going forth via any means of communication, including radio and video, the INTERNET, and literature. We promote teaching seminars, Bible schools, and correspondence courses, all aimed at winning souls to Christ and building the Body of Christ into maturity.

Bud and Betty Miller serve the Lord together as founders of the multi-vision ministry outreach, **CHRIST UNLIMITED**. The outreaches of this ministry have stemmed from a tremendous desire to see the Word of God taught in its balanced entirety. The Millers are firm believers in prayer and, through prayer, have seen many released from the bondages of fear, failure, and defeat.

Christ Unlimited — P.O. Box 850 — Dewey, AZ 86327 USA

The Millers have a world-wide vision for spreading the full-gospel message and teaching God's Word. Bud not only preaches and pastors a church, but is director of **CHRIST UNLIMITED PUBLISHING COMPANY**, an outreach dedicated to publishing God's Word in many languages. His experience, openness to the Holy Spirit, and down-to-earth expression of God's love have blessed many. God has endowed Betty with a rare gift of teaching that makes her a practical and effective "handmaiden of the Lord." Both Bud and Betty have hearts turned toward evangelism and missions, desiring to tell everyone of God's wonderful love. Their anointed teaching comes across with simplicity and in the power of the Holy Spirit.

The outreaches of **CHRIST UNLIMITED** are in obedience to the words of our Lord in **Mark 16:15: Go ye into all the world and preach the gospel to every creature.** This mandate from the Lord presents a challenge to our generation as an estimated 25 percent of the world's population still have not heard the Good News of Jesus Christ.[1]

CHRIST UNLIMITED MINISTRIES also is dedicated to teaching God's Word. **Hosea 4:6 says: My people are destroyed for lack of knowledge.** Many Christians are leading defeated lives simply because they do not know God's Word in its fullest.

CHRIST UNLIMITED MINISTRIES has provided literature for those who desire to know God's Word in a greater way. The main thrust of the teaching and literature is directed at "How to be an overcomer." In the endtimes, we must be prepared to overcome the onslaughts of Satan. Many Christians are suffering needlessly, because they do not know how to overcome sickness, depression, divorce, fear, and financial failure. **CHRIST UNLIMITED MINISTRIES** provides answers for troubled families as well as trains workers for service.

DOCTRINAL STATEMENT

> Jesus answered them, and said, My doctrine is not mine, but his that sent me. If any man will do his will, he shall know of the doctrine, whether it beof God, or whether I speak of myself.
>
> John 7:16,17

Inspiration of Scriptures: We believe that the Holy Bible is the written Word of the Living God. We believe it was inspired by the Holy Spirit and recorded by holy men of old. It is infallible in content and a perfect treasure of heavenly instruction which is truth without any mixture of error. The Bible reveals the principles by which God will judge us and reveals His great plan of salvation. It will remain eternally. We believe the Bible is the true center of Christian union and the supreme standard by which all human conduct, creeds, and opinions should be tried. Therefore, we believe this Word should go into all the world and should be given first place in every believer's life (**2 Tim. 3:16; Heb. 4:12; 1 Pet. 1:23-25; and 2 Pet. 1:19-21**).

Christ Unlimited — P.O. Box 850 — Dewey, AZ 86327   USA

God: We believe in one God revealed in three persons: the Father, the Son, and the Holy Ghost...making up the blessed Trinity (Matt. 3:16,17; 1 John 5:6,7).

Man: We believe that man, in his natural state, is a sinner — lost, undone, without hope, and without God (Rom. 3:19-23; Gal. 3:22; Eph. 2:1,2,12).

Salvation: We believe the terms of salvation are repentance toward God for sin and a personal, heartfelt faith in the Lord Jesus Christ. This will result in a new birth. Salvation is possible only through God's grace, not by our works. Works are simply the fruit of salvation (Acts 3:19,20; Rom. 4:1-5, 5:1; Eph. 2:8-10).

Body of Christ: We believe the Body of Christ is made up of all who have been born again regardless of denominational differences. We believe in the spirit of unity, while allowing for variety in individual ministries as to their work, calling, and location as directed by the Holy Spirit (Acts 10:34,35; 1 Cor. 12:12-31).

Blood Atonement: We believe in the saving power of the blood of Jesus and His imputed righteousness (Acts 4:12; Rom. 4:1-9, 5:1-11; Eph. 1:3-14).

Bodily Resurrection: We believe in the bodily resurrection of Jesus Christ (Luke 24:39-43; John 20:24-29).

Ascension: We believe that Christ Jesus ascended to the Father and is presently engaged in building a place for us in His Kingdom and interceding for the saints (John 14:2,3; Rom. 8:34).

Second Coming: We believe in the visible, bodily return of Christ Jesus to this earth, to meet His Church (Bride) and to judge the world (Acts 1:10,11; 1 Thess. 4:13-18; 2 Thess. 1:7-10; James 5:8; Rev. 1:7).

Ordinances: We believe that the two ordinances of the Body of Christ are water baptism and the Lord's Supper (Matt. 28:19; 1 Cor. 11:24-26).

Heaven and Hell: We believe Scripture clearly sets forth the doctrines of eternal punishment for the lost and eternal bliss and service for the saved — a literal hell for the unsaved and heaven for the saved (Matt. 25:34,41,46; Luke 16:19-31; John 14:1-3; Rev. 20:11-15).

Holy Spirit: We believe the Holy Spirit to be the third person of the Trinity whose purpose in the redemption of man is to convict of sin, regenerate the repentant believer, guide the believer into all truth, indwell all believers, and give gifts to those He wills that they may minister as Christ would to men. We believe that the manifestations of the Holy Spirit recorded in 1 Corinthians 12:1-11 will operate through present-day Christians who yield to Jesus (Luke 11:13; John 7:37-39, 14:16,17, 16:7-14; Acts 2:1-18).

We believe the baptism in the Holy Spirit, with the evidence of speaking in other tongues as the Spirit gives utterance, is for all believers as promised by John the Baptist (Matt. 3:11), Jesus (Acts 1:4-8), and Peter (Acts 2:38-41). The fulfillment of this promise was witnessed by early disciples of Christ (Acts 2:4, 10:44-47, 19:16) and operates in many present-day disciples of the Lord Jesus Christ.

Christ Unlimited — P.O. Box 850 — Dewey, AZ 86327   USA

<u>Divine Healing:</u> We believe God has used doctors, medicines, and other natural means of healing; however, we believe divine healing is provided for believers in the atonement made by Jesus' blood shed on the cross (Isa. 53:5; 1 Pet. 2:24). We believe divine healing may be appropriated by the laying on of hands by the elders (James 5:14-16), by the prayer of an anointed person gifted by the Holy Spirit for healing the sick (1 Cor. 12:9), or by a direct act of receiving this provision by faith (Mark 11:23,24)

MINISTRY FINANCING

> But seek ye first the kingdom of God, and his righteousness; and all these things shall be added unto you.
>   Matthew 6:33

We want to share with readers the instructions the Lord gave us in regard to financing this ministry. As this is the Holy Spirit's work, we are to let Him speak to the hearts of people as to what and how much He wants them to give. Quite simply, we are to share the vision He has given us and trust Him to provide for all that we need. We believe the Lord pays for the things He orders, and if He does not order something, we do not want to engage in it. Pray with us that we will stay close to the Lord, and that, in seeking His righteousness, we will be able to hear His instructions clearly as to what He desires us to do. If we do that, we know we shall never lack of the things needed to do His work.

CHRIST UNLIMITED MINISTRIES, INC. is a 501(c)(3) tax-exempt, non-profit church, established locally in the Dewey, Arizona, area.

[1]Barrett, David B. <u>Cosmos, Chaos, and Gospel</u> (Birmingham: New Hope Publishers, 1987), p. 75.

FOR ADDITIONAL STUDY

This book is taken from a course of Bible studies called the Overcoming Life Series. The entire series is a virtual "spiritual tool chest," as it covers a multitude of subjects every Christian faces in his walk with God. It also answers questions that many believers have concerning the current move of God. These are dealt with in a balanced approach and in the light of the Scripture. God's people are not to live frustrated, defeated lives, but rather they are to be victorious overcomers! Other books available with their companion workbooks are:

PROVE ALL THINGS - Christ warned that great deception would be one of the signs of the end times. In this book, instruction is given on how to recognize false prophets and teachings. Clear Scriptural guidelines are given on discerning the Spirit of truth versus the spirit of error. The book deals with how to judge without being judgmental.

THE TRUE GOD - This is a teaching on the character of God, explaining why God does certain things, and why it is against His nature to do other things. It differentiates between the things for which God is responsible and the things for which the devil is responsible. Our responsibility as Christians destined to overcome is made clear so that we can live victorious lives.

THE WILL OF GOD - This lesson teaches us not only how to know the will of God in our personal lives, family, ministry and finances, but also brings understanding as to why God allows sin, sickness and suffering in the world. As overcomers, Christians are not to suffer under many of the things we have accepted as normal.

KEYS TO THE KINGDOM - Instruction on how to gain authority in God's Kingdom through prayer is the topic of this book. Many principles and methods of prayer are covered, such as praying in the Spirit,fasting and prayer, travailing prayer, praise, intercession and spiritual warfare.

EXPOSING SATAN'S DEVICES - This book is a powerful expose' of Satan's tricks, tactics and lies. Cult and Occultic methods and groups are listed so Christians can detect their activity. Demon activity is discussed and deliverance and casting out demons is dealt with in detail. Satan's kingdom is uncovered and the Christian is taught to overcome through spiritual discernment and warfare.

HEALING OF THE SPIRIT, SOUL AND BODY -This book teaches how to overcome emotional problems, as well as physical ones, and how to receive divine healing It also teaches how to renew the carnal mind and walk in the spirit of life, thereby overcoming depression, loneliness and fear.

NEITHER MALE NOR FEMALE -What is the woman's role in the church and home? Who is a woman's spiritual head and covering? Does God call women to the five-fold ministry? What does God's Word say about divorce, celibacy and choosing a marriage partner? These and other woman related topics are Scripturally examined.

EXTREMES OR BALANCE? -Many Christians have hurt the cause of Christ through "out-of-balance" teachings and demonstrations. This book shows how to avoid those areas. It also deals wisely with the excesses and extremes in the body of Christ.

THE PATHWAY INTO THE OVERCOMER'S WALK - This book contains answers to the questions an overcomer faces as he presses toward the prize of the high calling in Christ Jesus. How can we be conformed to the image of Christ? How does the Holy Spirit work with the overcomers in the end times? What are the overcomer's rewards?

Please visit our website for information on how to order the complete "Overcoming Life Bible Study." Our site is also an excellent source for additional books and Bible Resources.   www.BibleResources.org

Christ Unlimited — P.O. Box 850 — Dewey, AZ 86327   USA

Keys to the Kingdom Workbook
Answers to Lessons and Quizzes

Answers to Lesson, Section One

I. Introduction to Keys to the Kingdom
    A. Authority
        1. Jesus
        2. The authority of Jesus
    B. Matthew 16:19
        1. In Heaven
        2. Every believer
        3. The work of the devil in our lives, or any other of the things mentioned in the expository introduction
    C. In order to accomplish the work of the Lord on earth and in order to live victorious lives
        1. No, only believers
        2. Being born again
        3. a. Must be according to God's will
           b. Our wills must be submitted to God's will as was Jesus' will.
           c. Our motives and desires must be right.
        4. Yes
           a. We were told so by Jesus and the Bible
           b. The Great Commission
    D. 1. Praying in tongues
        2. Praise and worship
        3. Prayer
        4. Intercession
        5. Travail
        6. Fasting

II. The First Key
    A. Praying in tongues
        1. No
           a. Utterance ranging from stammering tongues to foreign languages
           b. No
        2. God
           a. The devil
           b. He does not know how to fight or hinder what is being prayed.
        3. Spirit
        4. No
        5. He gives us "utterances" in our spirits.
    B. Yes
        1. "The Great Commission"
           a. Believer
           b. Yes

Christ Unlimited — P.O. Box 850 — Dewey, AZ 86327   USA

      2. Yes

C. We are given power:
      1. To cast out devils
      2. To speak with new tongues
      3. To control serpents (Satan)
      4. To ward off any harm to us
      5. To lay hands on the sick and see them healed

D. Devil
      1. According to the will of God
      2. Edify
      3. Intercessory
      4. Magnify or praise
      5. Knowledge and doctrine
      6. Witness
      7. Prophecy
      8. Blessing
      9. Sign

E. Native languages, or "our own understanding"

F.   1. Speaking or praying in an unknown tongue.
      2. Praying in the Spirit.
      3. The infilling of the Spirit, or filled with the Spirit.
         a. The disciples and the rest of the 120 followers who were praying in the Upper Room on the Day of Pentecost.
         b. The answer is any of the "tongues" mentioned in Acts 2:9-11.

G.   1. The prayer language gift of tongues.
      2. Tongues in which messages are brought forth to the church with interpretation.

H. If we ask God for something, He will not give us something false according to Luke 11:13.
      1. Yes, if they have been involved in the occult.
      2. Repent, renounce his involvement, and get deliverance.

Christ Unlimited — P.O. Box 850 — Dewey, AZ 86327   USA

Answers to Review Outline Quiz, Section One

1. Satan, or darkness — God, or light.
2. A spiritual kingdom.
3. Those who love God and accept Jesus as Savior and Lord, saints of all ages.
4. To unlock the blessings and be empowered to do the will of God.
5. Authority.
6. A revelation of Jesus and what the Bible says about the Kingdom.
7. Mark 16:15-18
8. a. Prayer
   b. Praise
   c. Intercession
   d. Travail
   e. Fasting
   f. Praying, or speaking, in tongues
      (These may be listed in any order.)
9. Speaking in tongues
10. Praying in tongues

Christ Unlimited — P.O. Box 850 — Dewey, AZ 86327   USA

Answers to Lesson, Section Two

I. Praise and Worship
    A. No
        1. Yes
        2. Heaven
        3. Everything, or in all things
           a. Rejoice
           b. Called
    B. Worship — praise
        1. a. Fear
           b. Worry, or anxiety
           c. Depression
        2. a. Deliverance, or freedom
           b. Righteous
        3. Battles
        4. Inhabits
        5. Prison

II. Prayer
    A. 1. Will
        2. Submitted, surrendered. or committed
        3. Motives — desires
    B. 1. Demanding an answer from God, or begging God
        2. Fear of bothering Him about something
    C. No
        1. Lifting
           a. Submission or surrender
           b. Desire
        2. Bowing
        3. Kneeling
        4. Lying prostrate
        5. Heaven
        6. Our attitudes or hearts
    D. 1. Anointing
        2. Laying on
        3. Speaking
        4. Agreement
        5. Name
        6. Fervent
        7. Lord's

III. Intercessory Prayer
    A. Seeking God on behalf of others
        1. Jesus

Christ Unlimited — P.O. Box 850 — Dewey, AZ 86327   USA

      2. Yes

         a. Judgement

         b. Sinners

  B. Yielding

  C. Intercession and reconciliation and ambassadors

      1. Draw

      2. Authority

IV. Travailing Prayer

  A. It is a manifestation of the grief of the heart of God, or prayer that cries out to God as a woman in travail or birth pains.

  B. Hearts and emotions

      1. Joy

      2. a. Godly

         b. Worldly

  C. Uttered

      1. Cleansing

      2. Other people

  D. 1. To produce spiritual children

      2. To birth things in the spirit for the church

      3. To bring "sons" to maturity

  E. 1. Grieving or mourning

      2. Weak or faint

      3. Bitterness of soul

      4. Birth

  F. Yes

      1. Lazarus

      2. Garden of Gethsemane

  G. Time

      1. Privately

      2. It will be sometimes loud, and people do not understand. They might be turned away from the Lord by seeing something they do not understand.

V. Fasting

  A. Voluntary abstinence from food or other things in order to accomplish something in the spirit

      1. Spiritual

      2. Lord

      3. Body

      4. Ministering

  B. Corporate

  C. Food

      1. A partial fast

      2. An absolute fast, no food or water

Christ Unlimited — P.O. Box 850 — Dewey, AZ 86327   USA

      3. Fasting pleasant food

      4. Fasting food, but not water

D. By consulting the Holy Spirit for a witness

E. Fasting

      1. Isaiah 58

      2. a. Spiritual

         b. To speed up things in the spirit

         c. To release finances

F. Faith

G. Victory

Christ Unlimited — P.O. Box 850 — Dewey, AZ 86327   USA

Answers to Review Outline Quiz, Section Two

1. Communicating with God
2. Continuality, even in the midst of trials and tribulations
3. On behalf of others, to "stand in the gap"
4. Crying, moaning or groaning
5. Grief — joy
6. False
7. Spiritual
8. Normal, or ordinary
9. Bands
10. An overcomers' life, or a fasted life

Christ Unlimited — P.O. Box 850 — Dewey, AZ 86327   USA

www.ingramcontent.com/pod-product-compliance
Lightning Source LLC
Chambersburg PA
CBHW081516040426
42447CB00013B/3246